GÉRARD CHALIAND

MEMORY OF MY MEMORY

Translated from the French
by Tito Cohen and Juliet Kepl

Gomidas Institute
London

This book was originally published in French under the title *Mémoire de ma mémoire*, (Paris: Julliard, 2003). It was translated into English by Tito Cohen and Juliet Kepl. The final translation was revised by Jirair Libaridian, Jean-Paul Rospars and André Demir. My gratitude to all of them.

The first English translation of *Memory of My Memory* was published in 2006.

© 2006 Gérard Chaliand. All Rights Reserved.
© 2025 Gérard Chaliand. 2nd ed. All Rights Reserved.

ISBN 978-1-909382-86-2

Gomidas Institute
42 Blythe Rd.
London, W14 0HA
England
Email: *info@gomidas.org*
Web: *www.gomidas.org*

In memory of Osanna

"These fragments I have shored against my ruins."
T. S. Eliot

CONTENTS

"LA VIE EST BELLE" BY GERARD LIBARIDIAN (2025) vii

FOREWORD 3

1. THEN AND THERE 5

2. THE SIEGE OF HADJIN 15

3. THE COMBATANT'S SAGA, 1890-1908 23

4. MASS GRAVE AS BIRTHPLACE, 1915-1916 43

5. BLOOD DEBT, 1918-1922 51

6. FINAL NOTE, HERE AND NOW 59

Hadjin

"LA VIE EST BELLE"

The writer of this book, Gérard Chaliand, passed away on August 20, 2025, at age 91, in Paris.

Author of more than 40 books in many languages, adventurer, poet, connoisseur of cuisines and of people, Chaliand was one of the most important geostrategic thinkers in the world for six decades.

In the early part of his life, he had little to do with anything Armenian. I believe he rejected, almost instinctively, the lachrymose nature of Armenian identity and the institutions that supported it.

Chaliand became fascinated by, participated in, wrote about peoples struggling for their freedom and independence, including the Algerian war, the Guinea-Bissau and Cape Verdean and other anti-colonial wars, the war in Afghanistan, the Shining Path campaign in Peru, the Kurdish struggles. And then, the Karabakh war.

Around midway in his career, when he had defined himself as a fighter internationally for freedom and independence, when he had witnessed so many peoples ready to die for these values and multiplying the value of their deaths by writing, talking and teaching about them, he brought his Armenian identity into focus.

He turned our history into a lens, a powerful tool to understand the world and the powers that dominate it. He internalized the heroism of his uncle who fought and died in the defense of Hajin in 1920. He relived his uncle's courage and struggle through his description, understanding, and support for liberation struggles.

Gérard Chaliand

His model is not the usual way to be an Armenian, but it is the way so many Diasporans have integrated their Armenianness in their professional lives; so many have used their Armenian roots and their reading of our history to escape the definition of being Armenian as a victim and to call upon the Armenian as a fighter.

He thus redefined the meaning of being an Armenian and living the Armenian experience.

With his unwavering and little-known support for Armenia since its independence, Chaliand integrated his three identities: the Armenian, the Frenchman, and the world citizen.

Chaliand loved life. "La vie est belle," he said often. He loved dancing to Greek music, sipping raki, reading Kurdish poetry, enjoying Asian cuisine, and countless other pleasures.

I have known Gerard Chaliand for 53 years. We met in 1972, at the entrance of the UCLA Research Library, by chance. He was a Visiting Lecturer, in the Political Science Department, I a graduate student in the History Department. As time went on, we collaborated on a number of projects, including the 1984 Permanent Peoples' Tribunal session on the Armenian Genocide.

A few years ago, when we had our once or twice a year meeting in Paris, Gerard made a confession. The man who until his last days asserted that "la vie est belle" and left this world with a winner's smile on his face, said he had one regret. He said, I have written and published more than forty books, on geopolitics, irregular conflicts, poetry, including my own poetry, on food and Los Angeles, and on the Armenian Genocide and so many of them have been translated into so many languages. But none has been translated to Armenian. I asked him which book he would like to see translated to Armenian. "Mémoire de ma mémoire," he said without hesitation. Within one year we published the Armenian translation of the book that was closer to his heart and mind than even his two-volume autobiography, written honestly, painfully but beautifully.

With this special release of the English translation of Chaliand's cherished volume, we pay tribute to the memory of a person who lived more lives than intended when he was born 91 years ago. In honoring him with this translation, we also honor his belief in living life to its fullest.

—Gerard Libaridian
26 August 2025

Memory of My Memory

Foreword

The memory of my memory is not what I have lived but what I have inherited. It is the echo of the past, the submerged strata of my story. My saga's dark beginning. The bloodstain within my clenched fist on the day of my birth the tragedy of which I was to inherit as a child. Something I tried to forget. This brief telling of lives beyond the confines of my own was written between 1978 and 2002.

CHAPTER 1

THEN AND THERE

Now that they are all dead, the time has come to remember. I am, whether I like it or not, the heir of a murdered race and of a country by and large erased from the world's maps. I long disliked the faces of these ancient women, clad in black, forever mulling over a past of woes.

With my cousin, childhood games were dreams of a warrior's revenge. Later, I refused to make an irreparable grief my own. Farewell. I was about to begin a new chapter, free from the tracks of the tribe and from the ring of women spilling their sorrow.

My saga starts with you, grandfather; we called you the old man from the mountain. You lived past your nineties. Every morning you would go on a four mile hike and you cut a fine figure to the very end. I wonder whether you and I had a real conversation, ever.

You could never be deceived when it came to facing the facts of life. "Money is something you need if you are to be taken seriously and if you don't want to submit." That could have been the sum total of your teaching, had I shown any inkling of listening to you. What remains in my memory is your demeanour: sober and dignified. However, I never established with you the tight bond I forged throughout my childhood with grandmother.

You were born, grandfather, around the year 1875 in Marash, in Cilicia, a province no longer seen on maps. Your father owned a weaving mill. He also owned a café where he liked to sit, sing and play the *saz* and the *kemancha*. Massacres of Armenians ordered by Sultan Abdul Hamid started in 1895. Your father's house stood in a Turkish neighbourhood. His neighbours appeared on his balcony and said: "If you abandon you *giaour* faith, you will be spared." Your father crossed himself; he was struck and fell. He rose again and crossed himself once more. His neighbours killed him on the spot. He left six children whose eldest you were, my maternal grandfather. You never related this event to me. In truth, the only past you alluded to, at times, was bathed in glory and good fortune. Your golden age lasted from 1900 to 1915.

At age sixteen, you moved to Adana, a town nearby. You would purchase olive oil which you then transported in a caravan to the town of Iskenderun. You sheltered your profits inside a wide belt: twenty-pound gold pieces and a few Maria Theresa thalers. You then opened a shop which was put to the torch. Every week your caravan of some fifty horses would leave Marash at daybreak. After your father's death, when you were twenty, you had dreamed of emigrating to America. With a friend you slipped as stowaways to the island of Cyprus. There, in one of those flea-infested inns where four to six men crowded into one bedroom, just like the ones I slept in much later, in Turkey, all your money was stolen. It's often so in poor lands.

You returned to Turkey and resumed your business activities, the only opportunity left to you. As a partner to a wealthy merchant, you ran a few food stores. Suddenly, a cholera epidemic unleashed itself. Every merchant but you closed shop. Rumour has it that you continued selling food, perched on a tree, using a basket tied at the end of a rope.

While leading your caravans in that region, you met my grandmother's brother, a surgeon, whose sister you soon wed. At the start of the 20th century, you owned the largest shop in town and became the agent of the Ottoman Bank, of the Standard Oil Company, of two insurance companies, one French and the other

British. It took a whole day on horseback to go around your lands edged by poplar trees, orange groves and tobacco fields.

Much later, in Syria, I was to gaze at those landscapes you had mentioned to me; the poplar trees were tiny and white; they moved me most in wintertime when frost crystals sheathed their branches, bare trees in a haze; memories of the unseen.

One summer, cholera broke out in Deurtyol, killing many Turkish soldiers. A local dignitary asked you to build a hospital, which you did. It still stands today and serves as a military barracks. You were therefore awarded the title of *effendi* which made you a dignitary. We have a photograph of you in a grand black uniform, a red fez on your head, a gold crafted sword hanging from your belt. Your face seems solemn, adorned with a bushy and well-groomed moustache, and today, on this picture right out of a history book, you seem to me quite youthful, you, the old man from the mountain.

The powerful of those days came to your house to dine and to sleep. Among them, Jemal Pasha, who later fought General Allenby at the head of the Fourth Turkish Army, and General Von Der Goltz, the Prussian reformer of the Turkish Army. The Berlin-Baghdad railroad was built then. In those days, trains altered men's destinies. Then in 1908 came the Young Turk Revolution. It was celebrated in Deurtyol as marking the end of despotism, the revamping of old institutions, and the promise of full equality between the religious communities within the Empire. It was a short lived illusion. The following year, massacres took place in Cilicia. In Deurtyol, however, the Armenians fought back. Long ago, my Protestant grandmother recounted to me all those events. No memory of defeat ever appeared in her stories. Her elder brother, the surgeon, had set up the defence of the town against a band of outlaws. The hospital my grandfather had built stood beyond the city walls and the surgeon had defended this forward position for two days, aided only by a few combatants. At the very end, as the only survivor, he kept firing his rifle from every window of the building to simulate a group defence.

Slightly wounded, he had retreated carrying all the rifles. A few days later, several thousand Kurds and Cherkess arrived as reinforcements to the attackers. The surgeon, the sole owner of a pair of binoculars within the fortified city, saw them first with the green banner of the prophet. About fifteen thousand Armenians lived in Deurtyol, of whom three thousand had taken up arms. The surgeon led the fighting, surrounded by some one hundred sharp-shooters who had to fire only after him.

The Muslims began the assault. From two hundred metres the defenders fired the first salvo. The assault resumed. A second salvo was unleashed at sixty metres and the flag bearer was shot. The attackers drew back. A quick sortie was organized by the defenders in order to recover any weapons.

As the siege went on, water became scarce. On the eleventh day two British warships appeared and the crews disembarked nearby. The besieged fighters imagined for a moment that they were about to be rescued. They would learn later that the crews had planned that short delay only to land and play a soccer game. On the twelfth day the Turkish Army arrived with its cannons and three thousand men. Negotiations began; the besieged men refused to open the city gates as long as the Kurds and the Cherkess, feared as looters, were not removed. The request was granted. The Turkish Army then entered the city and searched for its leading citizens. One was found and taken to Adana where he was hanged to serve as an example. The surgeon died later, during the great massacre.

A year later, Jemal Pasha became the governor of Adana. You, grandfather, had four years left until the start of the war and five years before the extermination of the Armenians. But you were not aware of what was yet to come. These were for you the best years of your life: money, honours, power and influence, all due to your efforts, to your entrepreneurial spirit and the plain fact that, as is the case with anyone who succeeds in a difficult endeavour, you did throw in everything you had.

After a few more years, it was for you the exile to Europe. You were able, as a local dignitary, to save your life and that of your family, and you carried away whatever wealth could be moved. In 1914, the Ottoman Empire joined the Central Powers. To the Young Turk leadership, the Armenian community appeared as a potential threat and an obstacle to the Pan-Turkish movement. The three leaders of the movement, Talaat, Enver and Jemal decided to eliminate the whole community in a climate made sombre by defeats on the Caucasian front early in 1915.

Beginning in February, the Armenian men who, between the ages of 18 and 45, had been inducted into the armed forces, were disarmed, regrouped and used as labour battalions. They would then be exterminated a small group at a time.

On April 24, as the Allies reached Gallipoli, the intellectual and social elites in Constantinople were arrested and executed. The order for general deportation was given and made known by posters and by town criers. In towns as in villages, the population made up of women, children and the elderly were given a short time to gather a few personal possessions before moving on towards a destiny unknown to them.

A few provincial governors—and this is to their credit—like Jelal Bey, the *vali* of Aleppo, refused to obey the deportation order. They were soon replaced. The long lines of deportees crossed on foot the steppes of Anatolia and the Syrian desert. They were decimated by thirst, by hunger, by the *chetes*—common law convicts specially assigned to manage this population "transfer"—and by gendarmes and Kurdish tribesmen.

Eighteen months later, the goal had been reached: half the Armenian population had perished. Some fled towards the Caucasus. Those living in Constantinople and Smyrna were spared thanks to the presence of westerners.

The old black-clad women of my childhood reminisced: those dead victims with no graves were theirs, their very own, for ever and ever.

I do remember.

Like a wave carrying terror, I hear the rushing of the Mongols.

The plains swell with horses mounted by masters of cruelty dictating their law not onto a like-minded human, but onto a totally alien, race. Soon we will be wading in the blood. Genghis Khan said: Men's greatest joy is to crush their enemies, to hunt them after having deprived them, to hound them after stripping them of their possessions, to see tears in the eyes of those who were dear to them, saddling their horses with their enemies' daughters and wives.

At first, the Mongols did not know how to seize a city, lacking the know-how. They then slaughtered thousands of peasants whose bodies they piled up at a sloping angle to reach the top of the ramparts. There were, I remember, some beautiful plunders, not in the eyes of the vanquished of course, but in the savage joy of victory when everything is allowed. The conquered luxury of Chinese and Persian towns open to looting. Baghdad with pyramids of heads and bagsful of severed ears dragged by horses in order to terrorize the survivors.

Nothing inhuman is foreign to us.

For four centuries, the life of the Armenian people, a religious minority, was certainly bearable within the Ottoman Empire which had its hour of glory and tolerance. They were mountain-dwelling farmers and shepherds clinging to the peaks of the Armenian and Taurus ranges, craftsmen and shopkeepers within the towns of eastern Anatolia, and caravan-leading merchants criss-crossing the then-known world carrying Chinese silk and Indian spices to the great western markets.

The onset of modern nationalism tightened the yoke borne by minority groups. In Constantinople, during the 19th century, the Armenian bourgeoisie of bankers and traders remained like their Greek or Jewish counterpart, wealthy but politically impotent. The crisis of the Empire, overcome by European industrial might, tended to harden the attitude of the Sublime Porte towards national liberation movements which, from the Balkans to the Orient, were reclaiming their independence. At the start of World War I, nothing seemed to foreshadow the planned destruction of the entire Armenian community, a crime since labelled as genocide after the extermination in Europe of the Jews and Gypsies.

Powerless and vulnerable, thousands upon thousands were herded: women, children and the elderly. Any female was there for the picking: young girls barely pubescent, mothers still enticing; female sex forever the forbidden fruit. License was granted to rape the women of the other community whom one could never approach or marry. A man could grasp and yank aside any woman weeping and yelling: he could finally let loose ancient frustrations, slit the throat, sever the breasts, impale his victim upon a knife. Men until then docile subjects became royal masters thanks to a massacre.

Long human strands moved lamely southward into a desert where only the wind claimed a presence. Heaps of the dead lay as markers in the night-darkened roadways as the stench of gangrene was let loose amidst the thousands of lying bodies. Caravans of demented mothers slayed their own children. Eyes gouged, lips slit with razors, pregnant women were disembowelled by laughing men. Some old men had horse-shoes nailed to the soles of their feet like donkeys; they were allowed to stagger on all fours before being impaled upon a sabre. Others, with their tongues cut out, foamed at the mouth, gasping in a silent and atrocious agony. Dwarves and village idiots from the surrounding countryside rushed in to participate in the final slaughter.

Go forth, brave lions, gendarmes, peasants, volunteers, all carnage is allowed. Convoys with no hope of return, with no other destination but to vanish like a blood puddle beneath the sand.

On my father's side, almost everyone perished: only two out of nine survived. The murders took place at Hadjin, a town perched twelve hundred metres high in the Taurus mountain range, a country of harsh winters and dry summers. As in the neighboring mountain region of Sassun, every man had always owned a weapon as long as one could remember. *David of Sassun*, the Armenian epic, relates the victories of insurgent shepherds. You told me that tale, Father, when I was a child.

"From infancy so great was his strength that, instead of wrapping the baby in swaddling clothes, he had to be tied down with an iron chain, the kind used to pull a plough. Upon his birth, his right fist was so tightly shut that no one could pry it open, no one, that is, except his own father. The child held, in his palm, a small pool of blood."

Eventually, David, in command of the Armenian heavy cavalry, which was famous throughout the Middle Ages, defeated the army of the Prince of Egypt, afterward exhorting it never again to set foot in Sassun.

My father's eldest brother, a lawyer, was *kaimakam* of Hadjin. The French Expeditionary Force sent to gain control of Cilicia, fell back when confronted by the troops of Mustapha Kemal, abandoning the Armenian garrison to its own devices. My uncle died there and then, arms in hand, when left with no choice, better to die that way. The tribe was crushed by events beyond its control.

Later, my father received a letter from General Bremond, commandant of the French troops, telling him that they had had to retreat due to the difficult terrain. He added that my uncle, the lawyer, had died fighting for the defence of Hadjin and that the General entrusted the care of the hero's brother to France.

Such war stories are familiar to me along with the prowess and war stories of the *fedaïs*, as they were called in Anatolia: Antranig, Kevork Chavush, nationalists and guerilla fighters following the tradition of the *haïduks* of the Danube and the *klephts* of Greece. My childhood memories retain images of sharpshooters wearing their black headgear, the *cherkeska*, an ammunition belt wound around their waist, and two others crisscrossed over their chest, carrying a long rifle, two pistols, a straight Caucasian dagger, and leather boots as soft as gloves.

Perhaps there lies the roots of my interest in guerilla warfare, "small war" in Spanish, that is meant to harry the enemy, with no materiel or supply lines to slow one down, relying solely on surprise, mobility and sheer physical stamina. War remains a passion for me: strategic talent coupled with the need for tactical action chosen by instinct.

I know next to nothing concerning my father's childhood: a few images of mountain streams where one can swim, of bush-covered lands where one can hide, of mulberry trees heavy with fruit (later we picked that same fruit together). He had a great familiarity with domestic animals, specially young kid-goats, called *ulig*s in Armenian. He was attached to his city of Hadjin.

Once, in one of my journeys through Cappadocia, I met a Cherkess from Hadjin. I asked him whether it was a beautiful place. This young peasant answered "yes" and assured me that it was indeed a very beautiful place. And that he loved Hadjin.

At fifteen, you, father, became an orphan. Your parents and five of your siblings were slain. You walked all the way to Constantinople where you found shelter and where you were able to finish your studies in botany and pharmacy. In 1958, I stood in front of the pharmacy where you had worked, in Tatavla, a suburb of Istanbul, until 1922, at which date you left Turkey forever.

No bitter note ever burdened your stories. The blood of your past was hidden from me. You were always a marvellous father. I would travel anywhere just to bring you back to the light of day. I remember telling you once of a tribe that moved along while carrying the ashes of its ancestors. You told me that you liked that. You know, I too keep carrying the ashes of our common memory, and you will vanish completely with my own death only.

Being the heir of a genocide unknown to the world and unacknowledged by the Turkish state, remains stuck in the throat as an aching shard.

Round the age of sixteen, I began hating the cult of past martyrs, a masochistic burden borne by defeated peoples. I decided then to turn a page and for a quarter of a century I broke all ties with my origins, to attempt a life occupied with the adventures of all human beings.

As I now take the full measure of the passing of time allowed to me and now that all are dead, the time has come to remember that history and to render to the ancestors their due and their reward. I salute today your desire to live on while remaining true to yourselves, things I can respect without sharing them. My way led elsewhere. On three continents, I fought with various people whose existence I shared. Perhaps, they helped me understand you better.

You now return to reclaim your place within me, in peace, at the very edge of all memories, and your tracks follow my steps.

CHAPTER 2

THE SIEGE OF HADJIN

In 1920, the French troops withdrew; they had been sent to Cilicia after the collapse of the Ottoman Empire with the expectation of a French Mandate over that region. The carving up of Anatolia by Allied troops turned out to be a mere hypothesis. The armies of Mustapha Kemal had been reorganised near Ankara and had headed southward. One of their objectives was the city of Hadjin.

I see on my desk an old photograph of Hadjin before World War I. It was a small town in a region then still called Cilicia. For the longest time, one had to hold the gates of Cilicia in order to stop any invasion. The population of those border areas, shepherds and ploughmen, lived in a permanent state of alert, holding on to rocky peaks like those of Hadjin.

I have always been fond of such "eagle nests" at the intersection of several valleys which they control, being at once places of refuge and launching pads for attacks. This town was one of the byways leading from Cilicia to Cappadocia where one could find churches and places of shelter, cut from chalky canyons. Long ago, I slept there under the stars. In those regions, everything reminds us of the flow of armies, of nomadic tribes on the move, the clash of hordes during which the mountain dweller unable to retreat is bound to become a prey. Thus was Hadjin. I will never set foot there. Why should I go pay my respects on the spot of a disaster now wholly internalised?

I can spy Holy Mother of God Cathedral which, on top of a rock, resembles more a citadel than a religious institution. On a higher spot stood Saint James' Monastery, founded in 1004, a convent turned into a school, a place of pilgrimage and festivities, so say the chroniclers, where once a year equestrian competitions used to take place.

In those days, in Hadjin, there stood two other churches of the Gregorian rite, two Protestant chaples, and a Catholic church. The upper and lower quarters each had its own bazaar, its *khan* for travellers, and public baths fed by the waterfalls of the Shadak. There my father lived as a child and would climb the mulberry trees after school; he spent his teen-age years at a college until the loss of his entire family.

Hadjin, paradise lost with the warmth and love of his kin, was suddenly severed like a head. You never went back.

After the war, a few thousand survivors from the Syrian deserts attempted to resettle there under the protection of French troops who, faced with the Turks' advance, decided to retreat. This is the story I wish to tell.

You, my uncle, were now in command at Hadjin, which you refused to leave. Before their departure, the French left arms and munitions with which you now planned to survive the siege of the town.

And here you are inside the citadel at Hadjin. Memory of my memory: seven months of siege, as my father recounted to me, before defeat and death. With the passing of the seasons, food and hope diminish. Slowly and in every heart sneaks the certainty that no escape is possible. The only choice left will be to die with weapon in hand. No quarter is allowed. They will slaughter to the last woman and child. Too late now. Nothing is bound to happen until, soon, the final assault. There remains only, circling the town, a tide of pure, sheer hatred. This time, your opponents across the gap, they too are fighting for the right to live as free men.

My ramparts are only decrepit walls girding a town shorn of any glory. I defend neither proud Byzantium nor Jerusalem thrice Holy; only Hadjin, capital of my craving for life, Hadjin, a free city.

I salute the luxury of dying with weapon in hand. Have you known the powerless crowds led to slaughter? The shrieks of violated females echoing in the dark yearnings of their predators? The terror of children whose loved ones have all died?

Here is Hadjin, up in the mountain, holding forth. Flow then, streams of grief, never again will I lead my people to the shore. For us, never again the billowing sails made ready for departure. Here, our land, so long tended, will receive one last seed. Hadjin burnt to the ground and smothered with salt like the ancient cities rendered barren. Remember Hadjin. I am the heir of a decimated tribe.

And now all we have left, as remnants of a realm, are a few acres of besieged ground. Now that the very worst is accepted, all we have left is to hold until the end. I remember, I still hold dearly to the promise never to yield, to the taste of the last bullet.

Remember the servant's status admitted as the norm, and the placid order of a world where the victor lorded peacefully over the conquered. A single threat sufficed, nay, the threat of a threat, so deeply rooted is the craving for safety. Henceforth, never more obedience to the master's orders.

I can see again Sultan Selim delighting in the fragrance of a single rose, after witnessing the impalement of a few malcontents. "Lie prostrate before me, your face in the dust, you dog, while I savour the world beneath my feet as a garden amidst easy waters. I relish my subjects' fear. Sever any head that dares to raise itself. Innocent or guilty, a severed head always serves as an example.

You seemed glorious at times, in your own way, handsome despots. I hail you, conquerors in three continents, gifted rulers, builders of exquisite mosques. Time passing, you slipped into a slumber, your Golden Age behind you. O, faded glory: having made Europe tremble, you are now slaughtering your unarmed subjects. Abdul Hamid, unsettled murderer, had violent migraines and nights haunted by terror. Perhaps his nightmares were of eunuchs stabbing him in his sleep.

Dust of the dust of your slippers, behold your subjects and among them, even more worthy of contempt, we the infidels unfit to bear arms.

I now point my rifle at you, whatever it costs. WE ARE FINALLY IN PEACE.

I still feel the grief of the defeated: the tribal circle to which I belong is sealed with disaster. All valid men have been shot and buried in mass graves, their severed heads heaped into pyramids.

At times, the whole world is nothing but a charnel house. All license is allowed. How could they gauge frustration, men who spent their youth in countries whose taboos are limited. However, in all groups formerly ruled by the Ottomans, the obsession with sex, at least among men, fills all the mind's space. All fantasies are allowed. Nothing can ease the burden of an adolescent nailed down by taboos. The prurient need of what is lacking, the thirst never quenched in order to free the mind. A massacre is an area of total freedom. The sinister game of seeking, looting and raping on the move.

Behold now the endless lines of deported women: Come hither, sweet doves, female nightingales, come near, black roses demurely clad, let me tear you apart in my rage. Demented, I can swim the fleshy pond as a herd of crazed horses rushing through a breach. I despise your forbidden flesh and I wish to fall into a satiated slumber, right after the tearing of all fertile wombs. Blood dries quickly in the desert.

Water flows by the poplar trees. The last shreds of haze vanish from the mountain crests. Where are the gentle mornings of yesteryear? I can still hear the shepherd's flute so burdened with nostalgia that one dives into the past as a stone made heavy by lost memories. Never again, is it not?

Finally, there is but one secret: to hold and to last. Long wakes spent watching the night while waiting for dawn. True heroism remains the fortitude to endure danger in the long term. It is best practised in the last resort, with your back to the wall, far from your base, your ships burned, with no recourse. More than ever, moral strength is decisive. When the stakes are high for you and not for your foe, you have, often, already won.

But you, my uncle, you are now beyond these considerations. Your fate is sealed. You have no more power over your destiny. All that is left is the courage coming from despair, when you must hold on and make your enemy pay the highest toll.

Thus, at times, some men are ready to die to defend the Thermopiles; those Greek soldiers at least died a useful death. As for you, you pushed back the fateful hour without altering the disaster. And yet, you see, nations do remember fondly those who dared saying "no" and then died according to the rules. At times, blood is the price one pays for one's self-image.

Memory of your memory. I now bear witness to the fact that in Hadjin, after a hopeless seven-month siege, you died, you and yours, for having refused to live other than free. What could have been your thoughts after seven months when all was getting scarce including water? The burial of your dead before they could spread typhus; the wounded, most of whom were dying for lack of care; the burden of the children, the anguish of the women, softened by the care they bring to all; the combatants, each month less numerous; the supplies severely rationed; the unbearable heat after the freezing cold; and no hope, not even of a flight.

Only the attacks can diminish the anguish of the wait, when defence remains the only thing on our minds. This is the moment of grace, when your foe comes and finds his death at the end of your rifle. We can, at times, in the evening calm, ponder about man's folly, but during the next assault we must kill as many as possible just to survive, helped by the joy of having hit our target and by the hatred of those facing us, a hatred fed by a thousand streams.

I imagine that, on the last Sunday, before the end which you know is near, you gathered all the valiant men:

"My compatriots," you said, "I have asked you here on this Sunday which marks the thirtieth week of the siege not to exhort you, for you do not lack courage, but to praise your determination. I do know that words cannot replace bread or bullets, and even less could they ever revive those whom we have lost forever.

"And yet, our nation, three thousand years old, was able to survive due to its commitment to our language and to its faith. This faith passed on through familiar words which give thanks to the bread and the wine, and to Him who grants them through our labour. Thus we remained who we are through the centuries and through feast and famine. We gave Christendom its first and perhaps its most poignant churches. Ever since, well before the grandeur of Rome, which we held back, and of Byzantium, to which we gave one of its most illustrious dynasties, we have survived all the invasions, borne all devastations, ploughed again what had been laid waste, and rebuilt what had been razed. When our kingdom collapsed, after more than one thousand five hundred years, we went on to found another, right here, and that one was able to live free for three centuries. Meanwhile, we sent our merchants to the ends of the known world; we took part, according to circumstances, in the crusades aiming to break the hold of the Muslim vise, whose choking power was well known to us. We were then defeated and enslaved, like so many others, and for a long time. We have become scattered on three continents. Now that we are hopelessly alone, without any hope of rescue, and without any other expectation than to last for a while, let us remember that our people celebrate yearly a defeat, that of the Vartanants, where a millennium and a half ago, our kin chose to die rather than accept conversion to the Mazdeist faith of the Persians. Some defeats are really victories, not that they appear such to those of us who endure them, but because beyond our own selves, they keep alive that which sustained us and for which we accepted to die.

"Seven months have gone by, and the initial hope has been replaced by the fate you now know. We refused the Turks' offer to lower our flags, knowing too well what death would await us. The last food convoy sent to us never reached our camp. For a long time, we have lost any communication with the outside world. Yet, up north, the Armenian republic has been proclaimed, and the remnants of our exhausted nation have hoisted the flag of our freedom. I wish this republic, gained through heavy sacrifices, a long life; yet I know how threatened it is.

"At least, our kinfolk who live there are free from any yoke. As for us, no hope is left and no need to feel sorry for ourselves. I want us to remember the terrible massacres our people have endured. Not a man, not a woman among us was spared the grief of losing a member of his and her family. Remember especially the convoys of deportees, women, children and the old, led through deserts to a certain death after atrocious suffering.

"How deep was their grief when, with no defenders, they faced the unfettered cruelty of their executioners? We, here and now, whatever the depth of our sorrow, when our bodies and souls are about to part, we shall not meet death as lambs butchered by surprise, defenceless, after torture and mutilation. We shall not watch as our wives and children are tortured. When the final attack starts, no one will fall alive in enemy hands: it is the last favour we grant ourselves and it is our last act of the will. Amen."

I would like to think that, before departing this world, you had a final glad moment with a woman beloved. In the morning, you shaved as usual and cast a last glance upon the world before facing the final assault. Shells of 105 flattened the last houses. The chroniclers tell us that four hundred and fifty combatants out of three thousand managed to cross enemy lines. As for you, your flesh and bones were scattered forever.

I owed you this salute, you, my father's elder brother, thanks to whom, today, my memory is spared those surrenders which allow no healing. I only know of you this saga. May my words endure and spread it throughout the world. Let me add, in order to mourn, the ancient liturgical chant of the Armenian Church, sung at Requiem masses. Peace be upon your ashes.

CHAPTER 3

THE COMBATANT'S SAGA
1890-1908

Tales of the *fedaïs*, those few thousand Armenians who chose the armed struggle in the last decade of the 19th century, are rare. Fighting went on, always of modest scale, against the Ottoman Empire or at the very least against corrupt officials oppressing Armenian villages and, at times, against Kurdish tribal leaders who extorted ransoms under threats of plunder.

You would take to the road in the light of dawn, empty stomachs in the chill of an uncertain day, just time enough to dismantle your bivouac, a pack on your backs, guns on shoulders and forward march. You had just slept with your boots on, under your coats, around a fire kept alive by one of the look-outs.

Walking. Walking in the stillness, the column of about twenty men in tight formation, scouts ahead, some clearing of throats, no wish to talk in the biting cold of the mountains at daybreak.

The men are walking. Walking here, in eastern Anatolia, which in yesteryear was Armenia, transformed by the Empire and by history into an ethnic mosaic. You have to avoid Turkish hamlets, hostile Kurds, and only come into contact with the few localities of which you are sure. At your approach the dogs always sound the alarm. There is safety only in the mountains, rest only by the cold springs where you can wash yourself, wash your clothes and leave to dry in the wind, wrapped on bushes, while you oil your guns and grease your boots.

No one speaks of idle times, for memory only records and transmits through tales those instants, often brief, when danger has to be met: how we broke through the vise of our foes thanks to the dark of night; the time when we surprised them in the middle of their afternoon nap; the execution of a traitor in front of all the villagers gathered for the occasion. the harried flight during a search and destroy operation. Yet idle times last longest.

Waiting and walking and walking and waiting. We have sworn to sacrifice ourselves: it was the gift that would enable our people to cease submitting with no possible response but to beg for justice from the very hand landing the blows. The solemn gift of our lives like an oath upon the Holy Book, like an act sealed by the sign of the cross.

We are few. Through France and Russia we have somehow, haphazardly, drawn our ideas from those of the Enlightenment and from the catechism of social justice. We are sure of being in the right. We are the servants of the people, its combatants and martyrs, the bearers of the future. We are young, strong of blood, vigorous of muscle, our heads filled with dreams and, for some of us, the aching craving for revenge, that of the slave finally grasping a sword.

I remember the poplars shorn of leaves by winter, as we walked upon frozen rivers so as not to leave tracks in the snow. Our steamy breath, only, in the icy air, and not a bird in sight. Sometimes, the wind and its white squall forced us to walk head down, eyes half-shut, in a blinding landscape. The men who knew the terrain were acquainted with deep and dry caves within which we could finally find shelter and warm ourselves in front of the fire whose smoke fainted in the night.

Fire and water were our sole wealth in those days, with the comfort afforded by arms. Those arms which, as conquered subjects, we had no right to bear.

I see once more the old black-and-white photographs and the Mossine rifles with long barrels, similar to the Lee-Enfields still used by the Afghans at the start of the Soviet invasion. Four rows of bullet-belts around the waist and two more criss-crossing the chest, like in Mexico, twenty years later, for Zapata's partisans.

The Karakul cap from the Caucasus, still found from Anatolia to the Punjab, and even as far as Indonesia. Mid-calf black boots with soft folds above the ankles. The moustaches: in those days, all men bristled with moustaches, Teddy Roosevelt, the Kaiser, Franz-Joseph, Clemenceau. It was a mandatory sign of virility. In the picture, the first row of combatants is prone, the second with a knee on the ground, the last row standing. All solemn and fearsome and almost all condemned to dying young. The brave man's mother will mourn him, as they say in Armenian. She will soon weep for the sons whose graves she could never visit.

Paris, Geneva, Saint-Petersburg, there the first cells, young men and also young women, often students, acquired, at the end of the 19th century, the new ideas which forever shook the foundations of Europe between the French Revolution and World War I, and the rest of the world thereafter. From both Armenias, the Ottoman and the Russian, these youths, propelled out of the provincial world of their birthplace where despots and mediocrity ruled. They became aware and cognisant of the new spirit of the civilised world. How could they have avoided the Enlightenment after the emancipation of their conscience? Evenings and nights were spent discussing what to do and how, with, as reference, the great elders, the historical precedents, the analogous situations, as well as the model fit to follow.

They then returned, at the turn of the century, to Tbilisi or Constantinople, with the aim of settling in the country. Homebound, they would say, homebound. The return of the native sons, intent on giving all they had harvested abroad. With confused ardour, helter-skelter, there was a programme and a dogma: the nation, liberty, and socialism.

More than half a century before the liberation movements of the colonised people, here you are, promulgating the same hopes and dreams, legitimate or absurd. The first partisan recruits are young, recent city-dwellers, instantly open to the ideas which most of the country folk will not respond to. As is so often the case, the first group of combatants, all lacking experience, is killed or captured in a few weeks. Yet the struggle resumes. Gradually, here and there, some cells take root and manage to survive.

In the mountains of Armenia, summer is as brutal as winter: white sun bleached rocky soil, eroded hilltops, narrow ravines where conifers sprout. Here and there, hardly a grove appears, and always, on the riverbanks, are Italian poplars whose foliage is rustled by a light breeze. Everything needs to be done at the same time: planning for security measures, for food and munitions, organising the volunteers, isolating enemy agents, striking and fleeing, and starting all over again. You will suffer casualties, bury a combatant when possible, kill a seriously wounded fighter lest he be captured alive. If you fall into their hands, they will make you wish you had never been born. Such are the rules of war in such a place. The wounded prisoner will be mutilated before being killed. We too gave no quarter. Those who had volunteered out of conviction are now fighting to avenge a brother.

Do you know the exaltation brought by the setting of an ambush? You position yourself at the right spot so as to be ready for the encounter, after having set the clock of death. Waiting and then waiting some more and you feel your heart leap upon first sighting the enemy. The solemn silence. That jubilation edged with anguish as the moment of action draws near while you can see them ever more clearly. Only a sword affords a feeling even stronger than that of aiming your rifle straight at your enemy. Sweat flows and falls down your right brow, the side where you tilt your head as you aim. So much toil was spent disciplining these stubborn mountain men who are always prompt to argue about the pecking order and always inclined to feel hurt in their pride; moulding them into a unit imbued with esprit de corps and a sense of co-ordinated action. All that we sneered at regarding the discipline of the regular army had to be relearned, right here and in our own way.

There they are: their officers on horseback followed by black uniformed infantry whose outlines are like silhouettes etched against the rocky background in the light of the waning morn. The refreshing pause they were hoping for will be denied. The first salvo shatters the silence with its din and its fatal surprise: the fall of the riders, first targets, the panic of the horses, the cries, the frantic search for shelter. Before they can regroup, half the unit has been cut down. You fire and you watch the fall of your foe. Aiming at another, firing again, seeing, shooting once more. Their losses mount. After a few minutes, the near silence in this canyon is barely broken by the wounded men's cries. We rise to see better. It is all over. This time not a single loss among our own while twenty of theirs have perished. We pick up weapons, munitions, boots, belts. We leave. Days like this are so rare that they will be talked about for some time to come.

All my memories blend in a fog during the mornings when haze floats up the peaks at mid-slope.

One human chain behind another, through a never-ending march: going up and down and then up again. Our boots creak on the stones and, despite the morning's coolness, our shirts are drenched with sweat under our backpacks. A hermit-like monotonous existence is interrupted only by sound and fury.

Sometimes, in the evening, when we light a pipe thriftily—tobacco being scarce—we happen to ponder all we have left behind. Even more if a man picks up a melancholy flute that brings back thoughts of the past forever lost.

The Ottoman Empire was then called "the sick man." Attempts at reform had aborted. Muslim refugees arrived from the Caucasus and the Balkans, while, as in Greece, other Christian ethnic groups were freeing themselves after a long period of servitude. The Bulgarians were so harshly punished for their uprising that Russia's intervention in their favour seemed legitimate.

The last forty years of the Empire suffered seizures, as in a terminal illness when the body seems in the throes of madness. The rise of nationalistic uprisings sounded the toll of the Empire and put an end to the then relatively tolerant system. The time had come to tighten the grip, to centralise, and to repress. The diplomatic intervention of the European Powers, which were meant to promote reforms and to guarantee the safety of Armenians in the eastern provinces, could only exacerbate the ire of Abdul Hamid, the despot who refused to apply the constitution.

A cavalry unit bearing the Sultan's name was specially created among the Kurds whose tribal leaders had just been crushed by the central government; the role of such a unit was to maintain order in the Armenian villages. As for the handful of Armenian revolutionaries, they endeavoured to organise the villages, fight all sorts of exactions, and, when possible, to make alliances with the Kurds.

The Bulgarian uprising appeared to some as a fit model for the Armenian Question: to rebel, to be harshly repressed, and then to call upon the Great Powers in order to finally obtain some reforms.

However, no one had the slightest wish to rebel except for the inhabitants of two or three mountain hideouts like Sassun and Zeitun that had enjoyed forever a semi-autonomous status. The huge majority of Armenians personified exemplary submission: the rich city-dwellers were well integrated and the farm folk were passive. Long-lasting servitude engenders a compliant state of submission. The Armenians of the countryside felt that the Ottoman Empire, diagnosed as sick, was no doubt such in relation to Europe; however, it still had, with regard to its domestic realm, an awesome power traditionally wielded in a harsh manner. The Armenians were not in the Balkans but in the very heart of the Empire, right at the Russian border. Had they gauged fairly the geopolitical facts of these eastern provinces where there existed a mix of Armenians, Kurds, Turks, Cherkess, with no clear ethnic majority, but mostly Muslim?

The inhabitants of Sassun, a mountain stronghold, the very spot of the epic told by the David Saga, refused, in 1894, to pay the special tax imposed by the local Kurdish chieftains who intervened but were defeated. The state spread rumours that all this was the work of foreign provocateurs. The Army's punitive expedition ended in a massacre. Great Britain and France reacted diplomatically and offered a reform plan. Sultan Abdul Hamid, after having isolated the Eastern Provinces by censorship, decided to teach a further lesson.

In the mosques, the mullahs denounced the plot of the Armenians, allied with the Europeans—the *giaours*—who threatened the Empire and Islam. In September 1895, the massacres began and lasted four months: Trebizond, Cesarea, Sivas, Erzerum, Bitlis, Erzinjan.

The mob now began looting, raping, assassinating on a huge scale.

They forced their way into a house; they were numerous; they meant to plunder for they knew there was wealth. It all happened swiftly. Violent blows, shrieks, stampedes, useless protests, terror etched upon women's faces. Daggers plunged intent upon silencing.

One wonders what wrath was let loose after a long frustration. They were seized by a frantic rage. To be the first to enter, to grab, to shatter, to ram through doors. They searched for the bedrooms, axes fell, locks yielded. Now inside, they slit the mother's throat, the daughters yelled before being dragged away to be raped as they shuddered in horror. Virgin girls, all. The men took turns and it ended in murder. They had long watched those girls passing by, with eyes downcast, always untouchable and promised to others.

Afterward, they would go and sit in a cafe to recount all of it.

In Ourfa (former Edessa), on Christmas week, three thousand of the faithful who had found refuge within the cathedral were burned alive.

Something in the public mood had shifted since news of the violence had spread. Those, among them, who disapproved of this carnage did so in a whisper. They well knew that all of this was now allowed. Tension mounted. It could be felt by small clues while the Armenian Quarter retreated within its shell. Nothing had happened till that day when the Christians had wished to celebrate the birth of Christ.

They surrounded the neighbourhood, armed with clubs, axes, knives, and it was all triggered by an Armenian who had been surrounded and wanted to cast a stone in order to free himself. There is a certain kind of pleasure to spread terror and to become at last the master. It lasted only a few hours. Enough time to kill at random, in bunches of victims, and to loot and rape. Those who could did find shelter in the church. The killers were just passing by the cathedral when chanting was heard behind doors.

"Let's burn it." They piled up the kindling, spilled petrol, and lit the fire. The wind was blowing and soon one could hear chanting turning to shrieks while the bells were tolling loudly. It all burned while evening was descending. No one could leave. The killers stood motionless, silently, watching the flames.

"Christ will bring them to life", someone said.

It was over.

There also were a few pockets of resistance: the *fedaïs* organised the populace in Van; in Zeitun, they seized the citadel and kept control. But such actions counted for little compared to the number of victims. Great Britain and France were moved. Gladstone pressed Salisbury in vain to act, but Russia was set against British intervention. The massacres, barely interrupted by the protests, resumed at the start of 1896, in Van, in Mush, and in other places. No one acted. The balance among the Great Powers was fragile and the collapse of the Ottoman Empire would have led to too many unknowns. Political inaction was replaced by humanitarian protests. Famous voices, Jaurès, Clemenceau, Gladstone, were heard to condemn policies which were always prudent when vital interests were not at stake. The crime was committed.

One hundred thousand persons may have been assassinated. Several tens of thousands had died of cold and hunger; more than two thousand villages had been razed; kidnapped women had been forced to convert. And thousands more had fled to the Transcaucasus. A quarter of a million, perhaps, were crushed by the Ottoman Empire. An immense tragedy, which found an echo in the western press. Who could have guessed that all this was but a beginning?

On August 26, 1896, a commando of twenty six Armenians killed the guards and seized the main branch of the Ottoman Bank in Constantinople, a stunning action decided upon to attract the attention of European nations. The capture of the premier financial establishment in the Orient could only result in provoking a shock, which became two-fold: while negotiations led to the departure of the unharmed commando on a European ship, the Great Powers, unanimous for once, demanded reforms just when the Sultan unleashed his populace against Armenians living in the capital. Certain neighbourhoods were littered with thousands of corpses.

The consequences of the commando's action were suffered by those who had not even tried to rebel against the authorities. When you cannot arrest the culprits, you inflict revenge upon the innocents.

I did nothing, said the hostage, nothing at all. Precisely, answered his torturer, you ought to have done something. More deaths, still, to close the period of the great terror documented in the *Livre Jaune* established by the French Government.

For the nationalists, the only recourse left was to withdraw to mountain regions while avoiding the terrorised villages. All became harsher. In Russian Armenia, the situation was hardly better. The Tsar's representative led a campaign of russification: closing of Armenian schools, confiscations and humiliations of all kinds. The sanctuaries of Transcaucasia turned into traps. Logistics were set up from Persia to feed and arm the combatants of the interior so brutally hunted that they only moved under the cover of night.

The moments of combat offer a unique kind of fulfilment. You dangle at the fragile end of the thread of your life and your luck, hanging on to your rifle, to your hunter's instincts, always under the threat of becoming the hunted. There and then you inhabit a tight sphere encompassing your entire world. The circle's radius is your rifle's reach. You rely on yourself, on your companions whom you know well, and, maybe, on the cross which you wear around your neck. It all depends on who can surprise whom. Often, they are the ones pursuing us and they are always in greater numbers. Minutes then turn into hours. Each careful advance which cannot be stopped seals your fate while the clock ticks towards night-time when escape becomes possible.

For three days we were lying in a barn after having reached, at night, a friendly dwelling, unseen by the villagers. We were about fifteen men regaining our strength while organising our supporters. Someone must have betrayed us, otherwise they would not have appeared in such numbers, so eager to ransack the village, having spent days to uncover our hiding place.

During combat, you think of nothing else. You invest yourself totally in the machinery of life and death where neither yesterday nor tomorrow exists. All has come to a stop, save these men whose faces you can barely see and who want your death as you wish theirs.

You try hard to aim true, so as not to waste your precious munitions. Sometimes, when they start their attack with shouts, you fire swiftly, by instinct, in order to stop the momentum of their advance. Otherwise, as you disengage, you now become the prey. I hope I have enough time to reload. The only focus of your mind is combat. Many times you will relive this exceptional moment with no yesterday and no tomorrow, till the last day when all will be made up of yesterdays and then more yesterdays, with no tomorrows.

It was then that very harsh years began. We had to make ourselves respected after the lesson inflicted upon us by the Sultan. The small Mazrik Kurdish tribe of the Hamidiehs, encouraged by the authorities, had razed an Armenian village in 1897. We organised a punitive raid from Persia to Khanasor to liquidate the Kurdish tribe, sparing only women and children. Successful punitive expeditions against troops or tribes enhanced our prestige. At the same time, we tried to establish alliances with the Kurds, such alliances always being precarious and dependent on individuals and not on principles. To make oneself respected, one had to return blow for blow, giving proof of more courage than prudence; they had to be made to believe that luck was on our side because twice or thrice we had saved our skins against all odds.

Every facet of our lives resembled a chase, we being both hunter and hunted. I have always been fond of the stalking of the enemy. To pursue with no rest, unseen, till the right moment felt by instinct which should not be missed. Set the trap and charge. Things happen quickly. Long hours and long days spent preparing the ambush suddenly become a decisive instant where everything will tilt. Hunter or hunted. A mistake will be dearly paid. Otherwise, the stalking resumes, and this time the enemy is breathing down our necks, ready for the close. He too has tried long and hard in order to find us.

Sometimes, we must use speed to slip through the ring of enemies closing in on us. Search and destroy operations begin with ferocious harshness. At such times, you may only count on your legs, your lungs, and your knowledge of the terrain. You fight one against ten and nothing is more arduous than disengaging after the trap has sprung.

Night fighting alone gives you an opportunity, if the moonlight is not too bright, to break through the barrier at its weakest point while deceiving your foe. And then, good luck. We know where to regroup at dawn if our sortie was successful. At night, you are roaring just to hide your fear and to frighten others. You do not know whether you have crossed the line. You resemble a wild beast, half blinded, crossing low-lying bushes amidst rifle shots whose aim is doubtful. We always leave behind our dead and our wounded fighters whom they will kill.

Your hand grasping your rifle, your breath like a forge where your heart rumbles, you rush towards dawn.

Once, I remember, it ended in a fight with knives. The blade increases your reach with the promise of death. Nothing is more direct than this straight blade which suddenly elects the one who will rise no more. At times, the blow is so violent that you only have enough time to see your adversary suddenly stiffen.

The most aching anguish happens when only a few steps are left between you and the other man with his curved dagger well in hand. The looks, the parries, the swift movement which, for one of you, will be the very last. The instant, heavy as lead, when you stumble and the opponent is upon you already. The slashing cut, cold inside your flesh, and the blow that you return right through his chest. You feel the penetrating thrust of your blade which, once more, frees you from your expected death. The keen appeal of a dagger's blade, its cutting edge, the crafted steel, the handle so finely moulded for your fist. The trusted point. May your wound be fatal; so whisper the fighters tied to revenge-vendetta, stretching from the Mediterranean to the Afghan border. The dark instinct which draws me to a knife is a tale of death, dealt and suffered, within the memory of my memory.

Weapons bought at that time in Russia transited through the Caucasus towards Persia and Van, which was a dispatch centre for the provinces. In Macedonia, we put to good use the goodwill of our accomplices in the arsenal, as was the case at the Military Academy of Plovdiv, where, since time immemorial, an Armenian minority had settled. Sometimes, we were lucky enough to obtain horses and then we felt freer and like lords.

The horse is the most beautiful animal in the world. We lived with our horses. From early childhood, we rode on colts. We love everything about the horse, its smell and sweat. We brush our mount from the mane to the hooves. We are one with our horse. My father told me that, if you want your horse to recognise you, feed him bread soaked in your sweat. You sleep against your mount, your wrist tied to the reins. In the morning, man and beast drink together from the same spring. The neighing splits the dawn and we hop lightly into the saddle, forming a dense group, as if about to enter flood-like within the Sultan's gardens.

No image surpasses in beauty of the lone rider on an endless plain.

My ears still hear the drum of the gallop on the Anatolian steppe. How could I fail to feel this joy lodged in my chest as the wind blows? I am wed to my horse's cadence and to the sensation of being the Lord of this Earth.

A group of riders descends upon a still world meant to be subdued. You appear like a scourge or like justice itself, but it is all the same. The gallop imposes your dominion upon them. The cannon alone can resist this rush, you nail men to their fright, you make the wind bleed.

Those horses provided us with consolation from the winter which we spent hidden underground like bears, with little food, much sleep, waiting for the thaw, our sole shelter a snow tent and our only wealth a brazier.

From 1890 to 1908 the Armenians participate in all the revolutionary movements of the Orient: in Transcaucasia against the Tsar; with the Macedonians against the Ottoman Empire; in Persia they play a crucial role in the constitutional revolution; in the Ottoman Empire they resist the tyranny of Abdul Hamid till the Young Turk Revolution, which they support.

We meet them in Saint-Petersburg, Tbilisi, Baku, Cairo, Geneva, Paris, London, Tabriz, Teheran, Sofia, Boston, Berlin, and Rome.

In Macedonia, at the start of the 19th century, the Armenian fighters train and organise the Macedonians giving them bombs and ordnance experts. In Persia, in 1906, with the Bakhtiars, they seize Teheran and re-establish the Constitution. On the side of the Russian and Georgian Mensheviks and the Bolsheviks, we find them present in all the workers' struggles from Tbilisi to Baku, at the beginning of the century. In the Ottoman Empire, they try vainly to propagate the slogans of class struggle and to advance the alliance of exploited peoples against their leaders and their abuses.

As the century begins, the Armenian parties demand in vain the return to the Constitution of 1876 which Abdul Hamid refuses to implement. Contacts are established with modernist Turkish elites, tired of a corrupt and rotting regime, who advocate an Ottomanism open to all subjects, capable of giving the Empire a second wind.

In 1904, the Governor General of the Caucasus arms the Azeris, then called Tatars, against the Armenians in Baku. The revolutionaries must fight on two fronts. With weapons stilled, the Russian troops hold back till the Armenians flip the situation in their favour. Soon the 1905 revolution erupts. The Governor General is recalled.

Among you, there were some individuals of epic stature whose lives, often cut short, were so full that they were worth a thousand lives.

Yeprem Davitiants was called Yeprem Khan. At twenty, he participated in the first group wanting to move from the Russian Caucasus to Anatolia in order to unleash armed struggle. He was captured and sent to serve his prison sentence on the island of Sakhalin, north of Japan. He escaped two years later and rejoined the Dashnak party to participate actively with the Bakhtiars in the constitutional revolution in Persia against the Shah (1906). He even became the Chief of the Revolutionary Police in Teheran. Then, during the counter-revolution, he led, for three years, a guerrilla movement against the monarchists in Ghilan. In those days, one could be an armed comrade in a neighbouring nation. Soon Russian intervention gave the Shah the advantage. Yeprem died at Hamadan, fighting the monarchists and their ally, tsarist Russia.

Carpenter by trade, Antranig was, at thirty, one of the famous irregular combatants in the Mush region. He spent some time in Transcaucasia, then, at the turn of the century, became the most visible chief in the *vilayet* of Bitlis. His prestige grew even more when he succeeded in breaking the siege of Arakelots monastery, escaping with his men dressed in Turkish uniforms. Briefly a member of the Dashnak party, he reappeared after a massive search and destroy operation, first in Persia, then in Transcaucasia, before being involved in Sofia in the struggles of the Macedonians against the Ottoman Empire. In 1910-1911, he participated at the head of some two hundred Armenian soldiers in the first Balkan War and he finished World War I on the Caucasian front, in Nagorno-Karabakh.

I recall Murad, born in Hadjin, who studied medicine in Geneva and was one of the first to join the Hintchak Revolutionary Socialist Party. He participated in the organisation of the protest march of Kum Kapi in Constantinople in 1890. In 1904, he was one of the two Hintchak cadres who attempted an insurrection at Sassun. He was arrested, condemned to death, and his sentence was commuted to twelve years captivity in Libya. Managing to escape, he fled to the USA from where he returned after the Young Turk Revolution. He was a representative from Adana in the Ottoman Parliament when he was assassinated in April 1915.

There also was Ruben whose memoirs are so crucial to understand those times. Educated at the Lazarian Institute of Moscow, he enrolled as a guerrilla fighter at the age of twenty two and soon was in charge of the Taron region until the Young Turk Revolution. He then began scientific studies in Geneva. In 1915, he tried to save, weapon in hand, the Armenian populations of Taron. All in vain. The following year, forced to retreat, he crossed enemy lines. Later, he severely suppressed the Azeri population so as to force them to evacuate the territory of independent Armenia. He opposed the extravagant territorial demands of the Armenian delegation to the Peace Conferences with the words: "Only demand what you can defend." As War and Interior Minister of independent Armenia, he crushed a Bolshevik uprising before the Red Army was able to bring Armenia within the Soviet sphere. He spent all of the following year fighting in the mountainous corner of Zanguezur before retreating to Europe via Persia.

Twenty to thirty such men followed similar itineraries dictated by the times they lived in. They were revolutionaries. Long before the Bolshevik Revolution, they fought as allies with neighbouring people, Persians, Macedonians, Georgians, in the name of liberty. I like the fact that they put their lives on the line for causes other than their own, just as the later International Brigades did in the Spanish Civil War.

Too many combatants fell. Comrades of troubled times who, in retrospect, seem to us—despite the boredom, the monotony, and the privations—to radiate a glory that no peace can bestow.

Yet I cannot forget those harsh winters when, at twenty below zero, the wind blew fiercely. From November till March, we, like armies of old, had to stay put and find, in a friendly village, a barn in which to spend the winter, hoping our enemy would not find us. Spring is radiant when all the flowers bloom in a few days, suddenly turning yellow or blue upon the hills, and the mighty waters bursting from melting snow rush down the mountain like an endless tinkling of bells.

Doubt, which often bites, also gave so much value to each instant that could be savoured. A halt during which we could nap granted us a few invigorating minutes. Cool water could finally quench our thirst. We plunged our arms to our shoulders in the icy spring water.

Sometimes food rose above the daily rations. We knew how to celebrate more than usually thanks to our flute, our drum, and our young bodies, hard as tempered steel. Constant danger, death looming above us more than upon other men, may have been the shadow of the happiness which we could dream of at a later date.

In 1908, the Young Turk Revolution, to which Armenian revolutionaries had contributed, triggered enthusiasm by proclaiming equality among all the Empire's subjects. Greeks, Jews, Assyro-Chaldeans, Armenians, Turks, Kurds all rejoiced and fraternised. The *fedaïs* laid down their arms. No one hunted them. It was a moment of grace.

As ever, it was short-lived. A new wave of nationalist Young Turks pushed the liberal element toward the opposition. Gradually, Pan-Turkish ideology replaced the Ottoman model. Beginning the following year, new anti-Armenian persecutions broke out in Cilicia.

Soon the Ottoman Empire began disintegrating: the loss of Libya invaded by Italy, Balkan wars which almost completely pushed the Ottomans out of Europe. Even the loyal Albanians, till then so tied to the Sublime Porte, opted for independence. The humiliated Empire reached the last stage of its death throes.

The issue of reforms in the six provinces inhabited by Armenians as anticipated by the treaty of Berlin in 1878 reappeared. All the Great Europeans Powers gathered in Constantinople and named two European General Inspectors for the Eastern Provinces. The Sublime Porte agreed in February 1914 and a few months later a Norwegian and a Dutchman were appointed. Never had the Armenian Question seemed so near a solution.

In August, World War I erupted. In November, the Ottoman Empire joined the side of the Central Powers. The Armenians now seemed as potential allies of the Russian foe. Though the Young Turk emissaries had been refused in July, by the Dashnak party, a request for the participation of Turkish Armenians in a destabilisation campaign in the Russian Caucasus, the same Armenians still fulfilled their duty as Ottoman subjects during the first months of the war.

The failure of Enver's offensive in the Caucasus, in January-February 1915, hastened the implementation of policies: everywhere in Anatolia deportation orders were published. The death engine was activated as the Empire fought on three fronts, at Gallipoli, in the Caucasus, and in the Near East.

From now on, the Armenian Question would be settled in the slaughter house.

Pathetic knights in a blind tragedy, all your hopes have been swallowed whole by the abyss. Unbeknown to you, in Constantinople, the project gradually took shape, trying to end it all, at once, and forever, slaying men, women, and children to clear the ground. This quasi-extermination, the first ethnic cleansing of the 20th century, took place on the harsh Anatolian plateau, where you had fought so long, and in the Syrian desert—and you could do nothing to prevent it. Deir ez-Zor would be the final stop for all those who had managed to survive till then.

We saw you for thirty years in a wide swath of the East, trying to change in the state of the world whatever seemed fit for change. You spent time in all sorts of jails: the Sultan's in Macedonia, Libya or Anatolia, and those of the Tsar, stretching from Tbilisi to Sakhalin.

Deaths of all kinds. The death of loved ones, father and mother, brother and sister, wives and children, compared to which, death in combat is a blessing. If you were caught alive, you expected torture of all kinds. Then came the bleaching death of memory of things forever lost. Yet, after such a hellish bleeding, with weapon in hand, you reached and preserved the patch of land which allowed you a future:

the shreds of a Fatherland where the sun glints upon the emerald colour of Lake Sevan.

You punished some of the perpetrators of the slaughter of a people and you cut down the one most responsible, Talaat. You did more than just preserve memory.

Your ghostly shadows parade down the white Ararat plain, riders in the lead, without fanfare, in the silence of the slow-falling snow. An army challenging a disaster, fuelled by the craving to persevere and to regain a stretch of land and freedom. Rare are those who, like you, after the loss of all, have snatched from Fate a last breath, a carrier of the future.

For you today the bells of the Armenian Church ring out wherever they scattered seeds of blood. Churches whose walls were demolished, whose gates gape, whose frescoes are erased, whose bas-reliefs have been defaced—but their bells toll for you, those of the cathedral of Ani, at Akhtamar, and in free Armenia. A chant filled with memory, which time, the bearer of oblivion, cannot waste.

On top of the secret garden, that of the heart, at the summit of the Sacred Mount, they begin to sound, as loudly as they can, those bronze bells of Ararat, celebrating the bread and the wine which you bequeathed to us. For you, through the light morning haze, the Ark has returned and stops in the snow, bearing the promise of a brave new world.

CHAPTER 4

MASS GRAVE AS BIRTHPLACE

1915-1916

For a long time, I recoiled from this chapter's trial. Hecuba, after the fall of Troy and the loss of her children, after losing all but life itself, perhaps only Hecuba, from then on sealed in the past, could have told of a disaster beyond repair. Which thread will start to unravel the skein, the grievous ball stuck mid-throat, the echo of whispers retelling the same story nailed at the bottom of my memory, the same images forever frozen at the edge of the cry? Mourning alone, mourning as a birthright, like a funereal lullaby, endlessly repeated.

The ancient women of my childhood spilled the beads of their sorrow, and while I played, the echo of their tales engraved itself deeply. Their narration, blood hardly dry, had been shed at a time when they were still young, twenty five years earlier, yesterday, and in my mind a distant epoch, for they had always been old, widows, orphans, in a world that had collapsed. And while I played on the floor with my toy soldiers, I kept hearing a whisper as a counterpoint about the death of this one and that other one. Your dead, mine, ours, forever, who did not even find shelter in a grave.

I remember one of them telling, while rocking to and fro, the same event, when suddenly her entire family had been lost to her. Her thumb kept stroking the key dangling from her belt, the key to her home, out there, in that ravaged world that had become a yesteryear burdened by pain. I know nothing of the brutal event she narrated. I remember her tragic face and her whispering voice.

They searched for weapons in the houses of the dignitaries. "What are you hiding? Where? Speak!" They beat them on the soles of their feet, turning them to pulp. They pulled out fingernails using pliers. Convoys of valiant men, chained in small groups, were led away on a march that would last one or two days. They were felled by sabres and cast into deep and dry wells. A general deportation ordered by the Government emptied the Russian border and all of Anatolia. They left everything behind: houses, gardens, land, workshops, and took only what would cover basic needs. A few wealthy men rode in carriages, the rest went on foot. "You will come back; this is temporary. You must leave because of the war; far from the front. No one will touch your property and you will come back." In 1915, Anatolia was slowly drained of its Armenian population in cities, towns, and villages. Forever.

Nobody caught on that a death machine was being set up. Who could have imagined such? You realise it only after the trap has sprung. The extent of a disaster can only be gauged too late. Each province, each city, each town, each village lived its final hours not knowing how others were dying. The convoys were assembled: women, children, and the elderly. The state deported its subjects deemed undesirable. They started their journey and died on the road. A death march to the Syrian deserts, guarded by civil servants, a convoy becoming, en route, prey to rape and plunder. Women, children, and the elderly whose bodies were left to the dogs, before they rotted in the sun. The priests were singled out; they pulled out their beards to burn them in public. They humiliated them. They were forced to go through towns on all fours, ridden like horses by thugs who spurred them on with jabs from daggers. They asked them to convert and when they refused, they had their hands and feet cut off before being put to death. Finally, they played with and kicked severed heads as if they were footballs.

Young girls and women were raped, kidnapped and sold. Stunned old women witnessed those scenes and covered their faces with dirt, amid moans, making useless signs of the cross. Children were kidnapped to serve the pleasure of their masters. Some, the very small ones, were tossed in the air to be skewered as they fell. Some of the executioners exhibited a special skill in this hellish game.

Like a dam bursting, sexual frenzy, after a long frustration, cannot be satisfied by mere rape. They had to, in collective hysteria, cut off women's breasts, slit their bellies, plunge daggers into live flesh before slitting their victims' throats. At dusk, women's bodies lying side by side resembled a flock of resting sheep.

Old men protesting or trying to intervene were tied in bunches to tree trunks and lapidated; they cut off their noses, ears, and testicles ("In any case, they are of no use to you"). Others were crucified and branded with hot irons. A priest who would not give in was punished after long torture by having his eyeballs yanked out; they then poured some gasoline inside the sockets before setting them aflame.

We could, till no one could bear to hear, tell in detail the horrors narrated by witnesses, the statements of consuls, the moral outrage expressed by men and women working for humanitarian organisations. The black and white photographs of heaps of bodies, of severed heads, of mutilated corpses. The entire arsenal of man's cruelty was here for display. Later, I witnessed with my own eyes, throughout the globe, their sinister instruments. We cannot for too long recount raw horror. We cannot witness a scene of torture with indifference. No book has ever listed the complete inventory of man's cruelty through history. Who could read it? Horror assails those who discover in the reading of chronicles the punishments meted out to the conquered.

One leader of a peasants' revolt had crowned himself king. Captured by his former lords, he was sat, naked and mocked, upon a metal throne as hot as fire. And the warlord who had been promised safe passage upon surrender was skinned alive and his skin was then sewn together and inflated to be sent to the conquering monarch. Wounds were smothered with sulphur to heighten pain. Slow tortures were repeated till the victim went mad. Others were impaled upon a stake up to their lungs, carefully avoiding vital organs so as to prolong the agony.

On the Anatolian roads, the convoys crawled by, women, children. and the elderly, and sometimes, those facing such a scene, showed some pity. All of this happened and cannot be forgotten, just as we cannot forget those who, risking their lives, hid their friends and neighbours; those who shied away from orders; those who refused to follow them; there were a few. At Trebizond, on the Black Sea, some were tied in bunches and cast into the waters. In the town of Bitlis, they were massacred on the spot. Elsewhere, some were killed on the road, and others died of fatigue, of hunger, of thirst. Some women committed suicide to avoid a worse fate and others did so after having killed their own infants whom they could no longer feed. What was arduous was not death itself, but what one had to endure till it came, while hoping that, perhaps, an escape could be found from a harsh sentence.

The convoys went by in the hazy heat. They went by in the wind-blown snow drifts. The fallen were left behind. The whip lashed at anyone who dared to stop. They trod toward the fall after which no one could rise. The guards pried away wedding rings and gold dentures from bodies left naked to rot in the stench of a mass grave, a sight much worse than the heaps of cadavers I was to witness at a later date.

As they got rid of the Armenians, they attacked at the same time other Christian communities: Jacobites, Chaldeans and Assyrians, or Syrian Catholics. Soon the Greeks of the Black Sea region were exterminated. The convoys of deportees converged toward the central provinces which became slaughter houses. Mass murders took place and the bodies were cast into the Tigris and the Euphrates. Soon epidemics broke out: cholera, typhus, diphtheria and dysentery wiped out whole convoys who had survived an earlier bloodletting.

A long suffering file was transformed in a few weeks into walking cadavers. After the shrieks of horror, after the violent acts meant to seize and despoil, soon nothing was left to be desired or acquired, except, for some, the pleasure found in torturing others. Here was a ghost column, another one there, and a third, and more marching southward; most would not reach the end of the journey. Mounted soldiers edged in convoys from which no sound was heard; they headed toward deserts in the shimmering haze.

This was not the first massacre. Twenty years earlier, there were those of Abdul Hamid, but, this time, it was no longer just a case of massacres, and no one was ready for what was to come. How could one be ready to disappear totally? This time, the goal was to end once and for all a problem which for half a century had vexed the Empire. This was a programmed extermination. Forward, march to your death, no one was to break ranks. War welcomed scourges. It was no use begging. One was alone, reduced to one's own frailty, as vulnerable as a civilian facing an armed soldier. Pathetic for being so powerless, forced into submission of any level, praying that it might be avoided, that it might stop, that it might not resume; all in vain. The bells of agony tolled. Nothing could stop shed blood but sand.

I think of you again, my father so beloved, of your family vanished, leaving you an orphan at the age of fifteen. You protected your last younger brother whom I later met and who was sobbing at your funeral, remembering those times. Both your parents and five siblings perished. Only the eldest son remained, absent, dead at Hadjin, weapon in hand, as I recounted. I think of you again when I remember here the catastrophe which took away your cousin Tamitza, with whom you were secretly in love, and who will be thirteen forever.

How could I still resent those old widows of my childhood, locked within the memory of their familiar world, suddenly blown to pieces? Could there be worse pain than having to witness, powerless, the torture and death of those beloved?

In February 1916, the on the spot massacres and the deportations came to an end. The last impaled cadavers were seen floating down the Euphrates. All that was left now was to dispose of those in the convoys who were treated less harshly, and who had ended in concentration camps in northern Syria, at Ras ul-Ain, or at Deir ez-Zor. For a while, some deportees thought that they had escaped death. But soon the order for the final solution was given. Those civil servants with little zeal or those showing mercy were soon replaced by those willing to kill for pleasure or by conviction.

Some honour and compassion lingered among a few within the group of executioners. Among the victims, some were traitors and informers, willing to do anything to survive. Some wealthy men paid to be spared ill treatment and were soon assassinated like the rest. An Armenian barber had a cache of poison which he sold, one gold pound per dose, to those hoping for a quick and instant death. Those in charge of the final solution enjoyed the sight of deportees fighting among themselves for a piece of bread. Soup was ladled out in tiny amounts and the drops falling on the ground were licked up and swallowed. That winter, the recent dead were used as blankets against the cold or as shelter from the wind. Some even ate the dead. Mothers fought to bury their children in order to spare them such a fate. The stench from cadavers was ever-present, mixing with that of survivors sick with dysentery, caked with their own excrement. How could one refrain from hitting and shooting in that human mass? In front of those making the sign of the cross, how could one resist shouting, as one of the camp leaders did: "I am your God; I hang, I kill!"?

Despite the shortage of workers, they managed to liquidate the two or three hundred thousand survivors of the death marches in July 1916.

Recently, I went through Deir ez-Zor where bones are turning to dust. A stone desert is edged by the Euphrates and resumes its gloomy extension upon reaching the opposite bank. The most wretched caravan dragged itself this far. A monument was built near the huge cave where thousands of bodies were cast away. I did not wish to stop there. The unburied dead tread upon our memory.

The Armenian presence in eastern Anatolia, formerly known as Armenia, vanished forever in a cataclysm meant to be repeated in the heart of Europe on a larger scale during World War II. Nation-states do nothing while tragedies unfold; only afterward do they honour the dead *in memoriam*.

There remain churches emptied of the faithful, whose bells have been stilled for almost a hundred years. On today's maps, published by the Turkish Government, they are labelled "Byzantine". Somehow, in that country, Armenians have never been present.

A few hundred metres from the border of present-day Armenia, in Turkish territory, one can see the Cathedral at Ani, formerly a capital, which to-day Armenians observe from afar, like a vestige in a forbidden zone, like an ancient mirror bearing a face long familiar but now lost.

Today I see again the old women from my childhood always clad in black; their eyes, now dry, focused upon a mourning whose ashes still breathe. The silent choir of things unforgettable.

CHAPTER 5

BLOOD DEBT
1918-1922

Yet war went on and the landing on the Gallipoli Peninsula turned into a costly failure. Russia had now become Bolshevik and had left the war after signing a treaty quite in favour of Germany, thus the major battles were fought on the Western Front, at Verdun or on the Somme.

The Armenians in the Russian Caucasus had exacted harsh revenge during the Russian offensive of 1917 by putting to the sword dozens of Turkish villages. They now had been forced to retreat by the advance of the Turkish Army. In May 1918, the Turks were getting close to Yerevan. The Turks' left wing was stopped but still threatened. The right wing continued to advance while neutralising, on its way, the villages and the region near Sardarapat where the Armenians would soon have to make a stand or face total defeat.

While the Turks' right wing initiated the pincer movement meant to crush their enemy, the Commandant of the Armenian forces addressed his troops:

"Soldiers,

"You and I can gauge our current position. We dreamed of a Fatherland on a land formerly ours, and that dream has vanished. Of those lands which used to be ours, we now occupy almost no territory. Or, better said, we do occupy some territory as graveyards where hundreds upon hundreds of thousands of our people lie unburied.

"Today, our backs are against the wall. Behind us, within a day's march for our enemies is Yerevan, where the broken shards of our people are scattered. Our future is now limited by the distance between Yerevan and the Turkish troops racing toward us. We are more than the last rampart. We are the last chance for survival. Need I remind you what massacres we face after each of their victories? This time, we have reached the end of the road. Afterward, there will be no more Armenia, and perhaps no more Armenians, at least in this corner of the world where we brought forth our churches, our chants, and the letters of our alphabet.

"Here at Sardarapat, this morning, escape offers no chance for survival. He who falters will be taken by the enemy and slain in disgrace. Remember that we are a people vanquished. For four centuries, we have lived as subjects, not free to bear arms. Our kin have been slaughtered in great numbers, if not before our eyes, close enough for our ears to hear their death throes. May your avenging arm also be the instrument of justice.

"Soldiers, no one is here to save his life, which, once defeated, he is certain to lose. We are here to save both the memory of our countless dead and the existence of whatever is left of our martyred people. We are the last bearers of the future.

"Each of you well knows what he must soon do: give our people a victory upon which its existence depends and to give ourselves the pride of having been other than vanquished. Let each man know that he embodies more than his own self, on this fateful day, and that he must fulfil his duty to the end. Soldiers, the enemy's advance must be stopped, whatever the cost. This is all I have to offer you."

That same evening, the right wing of the Turkish Army retreated. A fragile independence was proclaimed, whose chances of survival were immediately deemed very weak. The war was over and the search for survivors began. How could one gauge the scope of this scourge? Endlessly, names were added to the lists of names.

Whatever the statistical record, this state-sponsored massacre led to the disappearance of almost half the Armenian population of the Ottoman Empire. What number would that correspond to if applied to France or to the USA? How would this trauma be accepted? What emotions would be provoked by the denial of this "crime against humanity" as it has been labelled?

Who were the survivors? Those who, in great numbers, had fled to Russian Armenia and those who had been spared in Constantinople and Smyrna, so as not to scandalise foreign consulates and embassies. Along with survivors forever haunted by grief. On the Anatolian plateau, in the days of November, 1918, only a cold wind was present, and many bones bleaching with the passing of time, and a crime beyond repair.

Peace returned to Europe, but not to Anatolia. Only a brief pause during which an Ottoman court martial, in Allied-occupied Constantinople, condemned to death, in absentia, the main Young Turk dignitaries: the leading triumvirate of Talaat, Enver and Jemal, along with a few major accomplices in the massacre of the Armenians: Behaeddin Shakir and Dr. Nazim, who had headed the militias in charge of the deportation details and the ethnic cleansing on the road, along with Jemal Azmi, the prefect of Trebizond. They all fled to Berlin and Germany refused to extradite them.

The victors, British, French and Italians, now wished to carve out the Empire among themselves. A treaty, signed at Sèvres, re-established an Armenian state which could no longer be settled due to the human losses suffered in 1915. Greek troops, encouraged by Britain, occupied Smyrna, where there had been a Hellenistic presence for centuries, and advanced into Western Anatolia, without showing mercy. The Fatherland facing peril, Mustapha Kemal gathered around him all those who refused to be conquered. The Kurds contributed to this war of independence before seeing themselves stripped of any rights to their own identity. In the East, the Armenian forces, bled dry, were forced to accept the terms dictated by their Turkish foe, just before their small state was to fall into the Soviet sphere. In the West, the Greeks were soon pushed into the sea and Smyrna was left to burn. In this region, ethnic groups killed one another with a rage fed by ancient grudges, national and religious antagonisms exacerbated by the peculiar cruelty of impoverished societies, where a human life counted for little. Meanwhile, the sentences meted out to the Young Turks leaders were revoked.

The Armenians had lost all. Armenia lay under Soviet domination. Relations with the Azeri neighbours were execrable since the Baku massacres of September 1918, during the advance of Turkish troops. No Armenians were left in Anatolia, and those who, after the burning of Smyrna and the triumph of the Kemalists, left Constantinople, did so with a passport stamped: "No return possible."

Justice was not to be granted; the executioners were free and protected. The Armenians paid twice the blood tribute as they were crushed on either side by the Bolsheviks and the Kemalists who were now allied for convenience. They remained alone in a region in full mutation, about to deliver a new world in which alliances change to adapt to threats.

Rage and a desire to erase nightmares. Midnight awakenings with faces bathed in sweat and horror-filled. The pain of those whom we lost, whom we could not save. The immersion in a past when they were alive, before time exploded.

Thus the revolt was born. Time for action had arrived, time to mete out justice all by yourself. Punishing the executioners became urgent. To strike back at those who initiated the ultimate crime. Could one punish what was beyond redemption? The question was not raised. We had to punish.

At Yerevan, the web of revenge was planned. Logistical support set up in Boston moved to Geneva, to Constantinople, and Berlin was chosen for the first strike.

Stalking the enemy was a slow and organised job. We had to quiet the zeal of young recruits bristling to act with no delay. We had to locate our quarry and to try to infiltrate his network, to know his contacts, to identify his area of movement, and to choose the right moment. We drew a list of about forty guilty men, all condemned to death in absentia, among whom ten had to be killed without delay. This task was entrusted to the "Special Mission." The photographs of the marked men were distributed so that the avengers became acquainted with their physical appearance. Jemal Azmi, Behaeddin Shakir, and Dr. Nazim were located but Talaat had to be shot first. The stalking lasted four months. All the pent up tension was let loose on March 15, 1921, in Hardenberg Street, in the Charlottenburg neighbourhood where Talaat was cut down by a single bullet which shattered his skull. His killer, a youth of twenty four, had lost his entire family. A unanimous jury acquitted him. The determining factor was the deposition of a German pastor, Lepsius, who, during the war, had published a report, based on documents, clarifying the nature and the goals of the deportations.

So many years were spent waiting and nursing the craving for revenge or the burden of pain. The gesture to be performed had been thought of a hundred times. The physical presence of him who was executioner and who would soon turn into quarry. We imagine the drama and we grow restless. We dream of chasing after the other man, finally discovered, alone, whom we stalk, a pistol in our pocket, our heart beating like a drum. We have desired this instant devotedly. This face to face encounter when he, who embodied power, now sees his death in our eyes. For this second in time, this frail moment, we spent years mired in obsession. Revenge is a full-time job.

Operation Nemesis, organised on three continents was, without a doubt, the most extraordinary manhunt of the 20th century. It could have reached its goal only if a decision centre had concentrated in total safety all the necessary means. This was never the case for the "special mission" after Talaat's execution. Yerevan was now in Bolshevik hands. There remained, for operations' co-ordination, Constantinople, still Allied-occupied but less safe, and Boston, where everything was planned in secrecy. The theatre of operation was Western Europe where most of those who had been condemned to death now resided. On December 5, 1921, in Rome, the ex-Grand Vizier of the first Young Turk Government, Said Halim, riding in a carriage, was killed with a single shot in the head by a twenty two year-old avenger. As the horses panicked, the assassin, standing on the running board, threatened the bodyguard, and vanished as soon as the coach lost speed. A fine job. A single bullet for an instant death. No shooting at bystanders. Only the guilty man had to die, respecting the tradition of tyranicide and that of the Russian populists. The exaltation born out of the fulfilment of a holy task. Mistrust is endemic in clandestine operations. You must at once worry about your enemy and distrust your own men. There are those who wish to abandon the plan. Circumstances keep changing and handicaps increase. Luckily, on the spot, in Berlin, we had again a mole and we had already identified targets.

We could not let go of those we held by the teeth. We could not give up. Orders from Constantinople were ignored since Boston was firm in its intention to go on with the operation. We had to act and, if successful, we would be absolved and hailed. This stalking operation became something beyond the organisation itself. It was carried out for the memory of the victims, for those beloved by us, so as to enable us to go on living free of shame. We did it because this collective history had by now morphed into a personal event between hunter and quarry.

In Berlin, two young Armenian killers, helped by a minimal logistical level, would have needed nine weeks to finally surprise Behaeddin Shakir and Jemal Azmi, among a group of about ten persons. Both men, and they alone, were shot efficiently. Time had come to leave Berlin, the only regret being that we could not cut down some others such as Aziz Bey, the ex-Chief of Security in Constantinople, responsible for the rounding up of the Armenian intellectuals on April 24, 1915 and of the exterminations in the concentration camps in the Syrian deserts the following year, when he was *vali* in Beirut. And especially Dr. Nazim, as responsible as Behaeddin Shakir for the conditions of deportation and the planned massacres. Four years later, at Ankara, he was hanged for having plotted against Mustapha Kemal. All these unionists continued to be politically active. Jemal, for example, a member of the Triumvirate, had been named advisor in Caucasian policies by the Bolsheviks. A commando of three young avengers killed him in Tbilisi, Georgia, on July 25, 1922, in front of the Headquarter of the Soviet Political Police, the Cheka, as he was exiting the building.

Meanwhile, the most flamboyant member of the triumvirate, Enver Pasha, had chosen a tactical alliance with the Bolsheviks who confronted the same adversaries. In 1920, he attended the Congress of Baku meant to mobilise the peoples of the Orient against imperialism. He then switched sides and tried to head the insurrection of the Bukhara Emirate against Bolshevik power. Enver nursed the dream of a vast alliance of Turkish-speaking peoples. After a few initial successes, he met his death courageously on August 4, 1922, in Uzbekistan. The Armenians enjoy telling the story of a cavalry brigade which fought Enver's troops, a brigade including a squad of Bolshevik Armenians led by an Armenian from the region of Mountainous Karabagh.

In 1923, the Lausanne Treaty ratified the birth of the Turkish state. The Armenian Question has been solved, except in our memories. It was to resurface half a century later when Turkey opposed a United Nations report mentioning what is henceforth known as the first genocide of the 20th century.

In 1942, Hitler's Germany returned to Turkey the remains of Talaat whose mausoleum was erected the following year in Istanbul, on Liberty Hill. After the Soviet Union's collapse, Enver's remains were solemnly returned to Turkey.

Time has not erased the endless mourning, the empty landscape, the stones bereft of epitaphs in a wasted field which no monument commemorates. A territory of silent grief, aimless wailing, separated from the world by a stretch of several days of relentless marching.

CHAPTER 6

FINAL NOTE
HERE AND NOW

For many years I have been imagining these pages without being able to put them down on paper. Now that all have been dead for so long, and now that my own end is no longer far away, it is high time to remind the world of this mass murder.

Today, there seems to be no end to the celebration of victims. The status of victim itself is aspired to, though it has nothing to brag about. I have always hated the idea of becoming a victim, of dragging forward a tale of defeat. I better understand the "Never again" motto.

Words need to be inscribed. What is not engraved has no existence. This monument is to honour defenceless victims, as innocent as can be, humans engaged in daily pursuits.

The state having committed this crime continues to cynically deny that it was planned so as to end forever what used to be called the Armenian Question. Mission accomplished. This obscene lie is perpetuated from within by civil servants, lying knowingly, and from without, by those who to curry political favours give credence to a state misinformation program.

For a long time, I rejected this legacy. Why carry the burden of grief? Why wallow in the role of vicarious victim? Why commemorate disastrous anniversaries? All that belonged in the past. I wanted no part of it for I lived in another universe, my own, with a different history, which I shared with others; it was the basis of my new world vision and of my comprehension of things. Here, men and women share equal rights; there is no such being as the subject whom you tolerate kindly today but whom you behead tomorrow for having dared to raise his head. Here we can dream of unbridled love, and try to live it, without incurring tribal blame. The critical mind is encouraged and lack of respect is allowed. We have the right to happiness or at least to liberty. What happiness could be found in a state of permanent mourning? A mourning unknown to the world, of past events, barbaric, and almost shameful.

There was a whole world to be explored and discovered, other struggles, immediate, a present which one could perhaps modify, conflicts in which one could participate, the smell of gunpowder and of hope, in a world in the making, where so many people were freeing themselves.

For a long time, I remained outside this wasteland, but physically present in conflicts in Africa, Asia, and Latin America. Thirty years of field studies abroad complemented the western culture I had received from my father and from the schools of the French republic.

After the death of my parents, I felt the need, having participated in so many other struggles, to bow to this past history I had rejected and neglected for so long. It is just, finally, to accept the primal wound and to acknowledge its grief, for a final farewell. All ends in a rebel song, repeated from rifle to rifle, an invincible song of love and death.

Violence is at the heart of the human species and the rage to subdue is only surpassed by the craving for life, so ingrained that it often makes us slaves. It all hinges on our viewpoint on the universe: free or slave, rich or poor. Whether hammer or anvil, you will perceive a blow differently. We can, of course, rejoice in the fate of a species capable of transcendence through a work of art abolishing the passing of time. However, what I notice first is a visceral craving for safety: to survive and to ensure a life that will share with all animals the same intelligence, anxious, clever, and quietly cruel. The patient submission to the present order of things. Inequality based upon force or birth. Family, clannish or national prejudices, jealously preserved, only tempered by the laws of hospitality. Instant xenophobia and intolerance, only kept in check by institutions. Finally, war and its cortege of atrocities, of grief, and its ephemeral victories.

Thus the world has spun between the dull chores of the majority, punctuated by famines and epidemics, and the glory of the few sung in chronicles. Earth, where civilisations have appeared and vanished, where societies have been swallowed up, and whole nations massacred. And where, for so long, worlds were unaware of one another and became acquainted only through war.

Yet this murderous world is not limited to cruelty and madness. It also harbours love, song, laughter, dance, zest for life, beauty, creativity.

I participated in the history of my time on four continents. I was lucky enough to come out of it unscathed and contributed but little to the changing of the world. Whatever could not, or cannot be altered, remains so.

I do not share in basic pessimism and I do not believe in a golden age. Is it necessary in order to act to be assured of the validity of action, when what we love is action itself? I fought for causes which, in my opinion, were worth the struggle, and I enjoyed those times. I dislike nationalisms based upon excluding others, and even less tribal self-love, against all others, and injustice tolerated because it serves one's own group interest.

I harbour no bitterness—this sour taste so prevalent in old age, whose victim is the bearer himself. Why bemoan my fate? Nothing was owed to me. I criss-crossed the planet as others plough their fields, and the flesh of the world became my Fatherland of adventure. I bow to the logic of the world, where birth leads to death, as day gives birth to night.

I have been a lone warrior. A life so frail and beautiful, whose fires will soon be banked in the tides of memory. Yet calm is the bottom of the sea within me. Other dawns will rise when mine is gone. The steeds of the ancient world quietly graze on the endless steppes.

Paris, 2002

To Jemal Bey, Governor of Aleppo in 1915, dismissed for having refused the deportation orders and to all Turks and Kurds who fought such orders, in one way or another. To all those who would not be a party to the slaughter of a people.

> At the grocer Karabet's, lamps are lit
> the Armenian citizen has never forgiven
> the slitting of his father's throat
> on the Kurdish mountain
> But he loves you
> because you too never forgave
> those who blighted with a black spot
> the face of the Turkish people.
>
> —Nazim Hikmet, *Evening Stroll*

END

ABOUT THE AUTHOR: Gérard Chaliand was an internationally acclaimed specialist in strategy, geopolitics, irregular warfare, and military affairs. He was a romantic participant-observer of guerrilla movements in Africa, Southeast Asia, Latin America, and the Middle East, and he taught at the École Supérieure de Guerre (Paris), the École Nationale d'Administration (Paris), Harvard University, and the University of California, Berkeley. He had over 40 books to his credit, including volumes of poetry.

Born to an Armenian family in Belgium and raised in France, he rebelled against the "masochism of the vanquished" among Armenians, but later engaged with Armenian issues, especially the official Turkish denial of the Armenian Genocide. In 1977, he published an article in *Le Monde* on the "advertisement terrorism" by Armenian armed groups assassinating Turkish diplomats. Later, in 1984, he was instrumental in organising the Permanent People's Tribunal on the Armenian Genocide at the Sorbonne.

The Gomidas Institute published his *Memory of My Memory*, translated from the original French, in 2006. Chaliand stated on several occasions that this booklet was his favourite work, alongside his poetry.

A man who lived an extraordinary life—full of adventure and learning—Chaliand passed away at the age of 91, on 20 August 2025. This reprint of his work is a tribute to a life well lived.

Gomidas Institute
London
www.gomidas.org
info@gomidas.org

www.ingramcontent.com/pod-product-compliance
Lightning Source LLC
Chambersburg PA
CBHW031638160426
43196CB00006B/472